UNLOCK YOUR SALESFORCE SUCCESS

Discover a Revolutionary New System to Grow Your Salesforce Practice to Unimaginable New Heights.

PENDOWN PRESS LLP

An ISO 9001 & ISO 14001 Certified Co.,

Regd. Office: 3767A, Kanhaiya Nagar,

Tri Nagar, Delhi-110035

Ph.: 8130886000, 9650072927, 8595249536

E-mail: info@pendownpress.com

Branch Office: 1A/2A, 20, Hari Sadan, Ansari Road,

Daryaganj, New Delhi-110002

Ph.: 011-45794768

Website: PendownPress.com

First Edition: 2023

Price: ₹399/-

ISBN: 978-93-5554-946-4

Printed and Bound in India by Thomson Press India Ltd.

UNLOCK YOUR SALESFORCE SUCCESS

Discover a Revolutionary New System to Grow Your Salesforce Practice to **Unimaginable New Heights.**

ROHIT BHALLA

Creator of the 'Strategic Staff Aug 2.0' Framework

Worldwide Published by
Pendown Press

CONTENTS

Salesforce's partner ecosystem (that's you) makes $6 for every dollar Salesforce makes. How much of that money has come your way? *What was your cut?*

If your answer to these questions was a "Geez, not that much," then this book is just the thing for you.

It doesn't matter what industry or Salesforce Cloud you specialize in.

Through this book, I'll introduce you to a framework I call 'Strategic Staff Aug 2.0' that'll revolutionize your Salesforce talent acquisition and growth forever.

Chapter 1: Beginning of Beginnings (aka The Introduction)

I'm Rohit Bhalla, Asia's recognized and awarded Salesforce consultant and I've dedicated my life to Salesforce

- I live, breathe, and eat Salesforce

(to the point that I 'think' in Salesforce.)

I'm also the creator of the 'Strategic Staff Aug 2.0' framework that's helped 50 Salesforce Integrators and partners so far to grow by 7x.

But heart-of-hearts, I'm a coach first.

It's why I'm also fondly referred to as *Salesforce Sensei* in some circles.

I've converted my passion for speaking to business people into my work, and it's worked out great.

Although I have 8+ years of experience in Salesforce, it feels more like 16 years because I've clocked between 12 and 16 hours (nights and weekends) for the past 8 years. That might feel like overkill, but it's not. My guiding mantra has been to under-promise and over-deliver.

It keeps me up at night when a client hasn't been able to maximize their utilization of Salesforce because it's a direct cause and indicator for revenue growth.

"If they only knew what they're missing," I often think to myself.

1. a) My love affair and why it matters to you

Over the past few years, just like you, I've looked on in awe as the Salesforce ecosystem boomed and then boomed some more. It has defied any market challenges thrown at it and is still going strong.

In contrast, I see SI partners struggling every day amidst the competition.

It's a story as old as Salesforce:

The sales teams at Salesforce SI partner firms have no trouble closing deals, but delivery is challenging. They can never find the right resource at the right time.

Their brand name and reputation as a serious development firm take a hit.

Even worse, the firm may pull a resource from another low-priority project to make good on the deal at hand. As a Salesforce coach at heart, it pains me to see companies that should, by all accounts be growing, end up being stagnant.

I came up with "Strategic Staff Aug 2.0" to address exactly this crisis and I'd like to show you a way out.

I'd like to tell you that there's a better way to do this.

A way that lets you close as well as fulfill deals and increase your share of the Salesforce revenue pie. A way that lets you grow with the Salesforce ecosystem.

1. b) Why this book and why now?

If you have Salesforce projects on hand, but can't deliver on them because

- you don't have the right resources or
- your key projects are stalled, or
- a lack of resources stops you from taking on new projects

then, this book will teach you how to add new Salesforce resources and grow your business.

It'll help you finally keep pace with and even surpass the Salesforce ecosystem's rapid growth.

1. c) Golden nuggets that this book has to offer (read this first)

In a world where expectations run high and timely delivery is table-stakes, a hiring bottleneck is a nightmare scenario for Salesforce SI partners.

If for any reason, you're not able to hire the right resources, you're stuck between a rock and a hard place.

On one hand, you're directly in the line of fire for the non-delivery of Salesforce projects. Your reputation sinks like an anchor in the Salesforce Ohana. Salesforce AEs won't recommend you as a partner for subsequent projects either.

And the spiral effect continues into the next year with a difficult sales cycle. Growth tanks further, and existing resources leave as you fight fires and low online ratings on B2B review platforms.

On the other hand, if a project gets stalled, existing clients move elsewhere with their projects. Long-standing, bread-and-butter client relationships are severed.

This nightmare could play out at your business. It could happen to you one fateful evening, just as it did to Andrew, a delivery manager at ACME, LLC *(Names changed to protect privacy)*.

His story resonates with delivery managers the world over and touches a raw nerve.

Chapter 2: The Dark Evening

It's 7 in the evening and Andrew, ACME's delivery manager, is more restless than he's ever been.

Tomorrow, the status update of his project is due and things are looking messy. The project isn't on track to be finished on time.

To get by till now, he has stalled the management team by telling them the project is in motion and making progress. But, no more.

The project delivery date draws near and he has been called on to submit a formal report and update senior managers on the project status.

Andrew sinks into his chair.
It all comes back to him.

Feeling defeated, he remembers compromises made when hiring the team and lets out a sigh.

The next morning, as he enters the boardroom to meet the management panel and submit the report, he confesses. He tells them he failed to deliver on time.

Disappointed, the panel looks at him and contemplates how this will affect them.

Mike, the delivery head, reassures everyone that it was alright and that he knew of Andrew's great track record. He'll apprise the client of the situation and see how to make things right for them. He now insists on getting to the bottom of the problem to see why this happened.

Andrew and Mike sit down to discuss what went wrong. They find that when a resourcing partner was hired, they fell for tall claims made by the resource consultant who hid many things from them and indulged in malpractices like shadowing resources.

But Andrew and the firm have never noticed this because they have been under huge project delivery pressures from all sides. They succumbed to pressure and rushed their resourcing partnership.

They realize they haven't communicated freely or followed the best practice for hiring.

Andrew and Mike now know what went wrong.

It's now a year later. Andrew is awarded at the company's annual ceremony for quality and timely project deliveries. He's turned around the company.

The management asks him what's changed.

Andrew replies, "The success of our company depends on people, and hiring the right people depends on choosing the right strategic partner."

After hearing Andrew's statement, everyone is now looking at him with pride and awe. But there's a lesson for all to learn from his mistakes.

It wasn't an easy process for him to reach this level, so he followed some strategies.

Most importantly, he actually found out the root cause which we are going to talk about in our next chapter.

The key takeaways here are:

- Wrong team resources can impact your success.
- Not having the right talent can impact delivery which ends up failing commitments.
- Do not try to fix something which is not actually a problem.
- Having the wrong talent in the team can build frustration among key employees.
- Wrong talent resources cause bad delivery, which in turn, causes a loss of funds, trust, and reputation.
- Talent partners make tall claims, check them.
- Malpractices by a Small SI partner can sink project delivery. Insist on more visibility.
- Teams don't communicate freely under pressure.
- Due diligence is important when hiring strategic partners.

THE DARK EVENING

Chapter 3: The Invisible Cost

This chapter builds on chapter 1 - and talks about the cost SI partners are paying which they are not aware of, but bites them in the future. These goof-ups will result in a loss of projects and a decline in the growth of the company.

I hope you've read the last chapter, 'The Dark Evening.'

Today, 75% of SI partners see a 'dark evening' at least once in any of the months of the year. This impacts the overall growth of your firm.

But the problem isn't these 'The Dark Evening' events.

Don't let them distract you from the real problem.

Today, SI partners globally face several issues, like:

- Stalled delivery
- No repeat patronage from existing clients
- Poor client impressions
- Bad architecture
- Bad tech skills
- Stagnant growth
- Unnecessary pressure on key resources
- Attrition of key team members
- Brand reputation

All these problems levy an insidious, invisible cost that runs into millions of dollars (or even billions worldwide). At times, this cost is even more than the actual cost of a project.

ACME LLC, had a project worth 15 million with 200 people working on it. Despite this, they couldn't deliver on time. Consequently, the respect they commanded and their credentials in project delivery took a hit. The company's reputation has been in freefall ever since .

Their performance has hit a rocky patch, and at this rate, they could even exit the market in a few years.

Not having the right people at the right time is not something a bird's eye view will tell you. The 'invisibility' of this cost is precisely what makes it so dangerous. It creeps up on a company and accumulates over time while everything on the surface looks healthy.

The issue isn't that people don't know about this problem. Heck, this is a problem that's been around as long as the service industry. The is issue that despite knowing, people at these companies waste time solving the wrong problem. They only focus on getting people onboard and filling up teams.

That's what kills them.

As an analogy, an SI partner may know it needs 300 people, but it may not know it needs 30-40-star performers instead that can run circles around 300 average people. Steve Jobs knew this, and so should you.

It's this trade-off between team size, structure, and expertise that firms mess up. It's the configuration of these teams that's so hard to get right.

They also lose brand reputation and trust which results directly in a loss of business.

Put too many A-players in a not-so-demanding project and the cost balloons up, which affects revenue. Too many mediocre team members and the delivery never happens.

The issue isn't just that SI partners can't find the right talent, but that they don't even consider team configuration a major problem.

Let's enumerate all invisible costs that you bear.

Below are the key cost contributors which eat into your budget without you ever even realizing it.

Mismatched Talent

There's no way around this.

If a resource doesn't have the skillset demanded by the project, then that resource is just wrong and bound to waste everyone's time with unnecessary research. This research takes time you don't have, stretches delivery timelines, and inflates project costs.

Frequent Change in Resources

Resource planning is important before kick-off because it takes time to fully assimilate a resource into a project. If we change the resource in the middle of the project, then there's always knowledge to be transferred and dependencies created over time that need to be addressed – both things take time.

Replacement resources need time to understand complex project architecture and may also not think on lines of the previous resource, which increases conflict.

This is almost like restarting projects from scratch. Changes in resources too frequently aren't in favor of a project and your budget may go up in flames.

Delays in Hiring the Right Talent

Time is money for you as an SI partner, so if you have resources on the bench with skills that don't match the project, then you are wasting money on that bench resource. Looking for another  resource from the market at this juncture will only delay your project, which will cost you again.

Misfit Team Structures

Say, your project needs a diverse team with different roles to come together like Project Managers, Business Analysts, Developers, UI Developers, Quality Assurance Engineers, Dev Ops Engineers, and Release Managers.

In such an inter-dependent project, where one task affects the other, the lack of any one type of resource can halt the entire project. And a sloppy replacement will have to learn the missing skill (which takes its own time) or will deliver poorly on quality, which affects the rest of the project cycle.

Stalled Deliveries

The client may not have the patience to understand delays in projects due to an internal lack of specialized resources and they could take the project elsewhere.

Worse, they could parallelly give the project to other partners if they grow doubtful of your abilities.

They may even grudge you for picking up a project with a lack of resources which could dent your reputation and show up in poor reviews on online forums.

Other clients with similar requirements will be spooked by this too because online reviews live forever.

Like the Dunning-Kruger effect tells us, we can't fix mistakes that we don't know to exist and this may give us an inflated sense of our abilities.

There are so many areas where we burn money that aren't visible to us, so we don't give them enough attention.

I hope you get what I am pointing out. Now is the right time to look at it so that you can identify the problem and can start fixing it.

You may be tempted at this point to swing into action and grab the bull by its horns. You'll try to solve this with regular solutions, which you think are right, but actually aren't.

Allow me to expand on this in the next chapter.

Chapter 4: The Right Solution which is Not-so-right

You are now aware of the invisible cost which impacts your success but is notoriously hard to calculate. In this chapter, we discuss solutions that you may think are right, but actually, are wrong.

Otherwise, these solutions could have given you and every other Salesforce partner boundless success in the ecosystem.

As I've said in Chapter 3, the problem I highlighted earlier isn't new and SI firms have turned to a few different methods to solve these:

- Hiring Freelancers
- Building in-house teams
- Hiring from Small Shops

All of these solutions suffer from their own unique and fatal problems that may not be immediately apparent at times but can jeopardize your project completely.

Hiring Freelancers

This might be the first solution to come to mind, so let me walk you through some unexamined beliefs.

You can't expect a single person with finite attention to be dedicated to your project if they're dealing with multiple projects simultaneously.

Also, as lone individuals, their skills and availability are just as limited as them. They get easily side-tracked by other projects and new opportunities and require constant supervision to keep their eye on the prize.

The project never gets undivided attention and you're never a top priority for them.

This solution might sound good on paper, but the most you are getting is a quick fix and another loose end that's bad for you in the long term.

Building In-house Teams

This is a time-intensive process that can take upwards of 4-6 months for each resource, based on what you train them for.

And don't even get me started on candidate joining.

Even finding trainable candidates with the right aptitude for certain tasks is a miracle. Unless you've been lying under a rock, you should know there's an intense war for talent to even lap up entry-level resources.

Then, there's the high cost of hiring and indirect expenses for joining like insurance, bonuses, allowances, and miscellaneous expenditure to just keep the lights on and scale infrastructure.

Worst of all, if you're even the least bit inexperienced at hiring, you could be flying blind and hiring non-performing resources at face value.

You may be hiring without visibility into the pipeline of incoming work into the ecosystem and fresh talent joining the workforce. These have to be timed well and need you to understand the pulse of the market.

Hiring from Small Shops

After the horror of hiring agencies and freelancers, you may be looking for solutions within the family.

You may be tempted to form a symbiotic relationship with a smaller SI partner. We can understand. We all start somewhere and you'd be okay giving a chance to a smaller partner.

But as sensible as that sounds, it is just as big of an issue.

Remember, 75% of agencies are facing common problems. What if the firm you partner up with faces similar issues? It would be just more of the same with them.

A smaller SI partner will have fewer resources and a smaller available bench pool to draw from. It also won't have enough variety or advanced certifications. This causes its own problems. Most resources may be busy, so shadow resourcing and inflating timesheets are only too common.

A firm this size may also not have the means to conduct thorough background checks and upskilling programs. It may be sitting on non-performing resources and its own stalled projects. This may cause reluctance to provide resources and the firm may want to hoard them for their own opportunities.

They may also be new to the ecosystem and may not have holistic cloud expertise or skilled resources.

Worst of all, (a few if not all) may be too eager to grow and lack integrity. So, they may not agree to white-labeling or may even poach your hard-earned clients from you.

THE RIGHT SOLUTION WHICH IS NOT-SO-RIGHT

Chapter 5: SSA 2.0 - The Secret Weapon

I am sure that you must have learned something from Andrew's failure, identified the invisible cost which is impacting his success, and finally seen why solutions that are considered 'right' are actually wrong.

In this chapter, we are going to lay the foundation for the secret weapon that will change your eye lens and help you see the real problem which needs fixing to unlock success and growth.

You might ask, what are the solutions required to get the results that Andrew got after a year of struggle? That's exactly what you'll learn in this chapter.

If you want new, different results for your business, you'll need to change your approach radically. What got you here, won't get you there and you need to shift your lens to see properly.

When you hear the partner ecosystem makes 6 dollars for every dollar Salesforce makes, ask yourself, where do you stand in that ratio? Then identify what your real struggle is, just like I have specified in my previous chapters.

What you really need is the right people, at the right time, for the right task. In other words, you'll need to get the resource configuration right.

So, the secret weapon is very simple which we might ignore or not give the required attention – it is simply the "Right Configuration".

The right configuration is as simple as a doctor prescribing the right medicine for the right diagnosis. Here you need to play the role of a doctor where you need to understand the project's requirements holistically and suggest a configuration accordingly.

If you understand the capabilities of the resources you have vis-a-vis the project demands and you align them with the client's shared goals, you'll find immense and repeatable success for all projects.

Assigning the Right Talent or Resource to the Right project is the 'Right Configuration.' It's only once you arrive at the right configuration that you'll deliver quality projects on time.

There are many varieties and possibilities of teams you can build. You'll either need to learn these configurations with time or get a strategic partner on your side that can advise you on this and care for your global strategic vision. For what it's worth, a hiring agency that has a purely transactional, resource-for-money relationship simply won't cut it.

And beware, if such a strategy is not built on the right framework, the entire operation falls apart very quickly.

If you don't learn from the history of Andrew, you'll be history yourself. The one and only framework that can save you from this fate is called – "Strategic Staff Augmentation 2.0".

Andrew discovered it, implemented it, and resolved his challenges faster than he could think. It worked wonderfully for him and it can work wonders for you as well.

This begs the question, what really even is Strategic Staff Augmentation 2.0? And how different it is from the framework that you use for staff augmentation?

Let's answer this with another question.

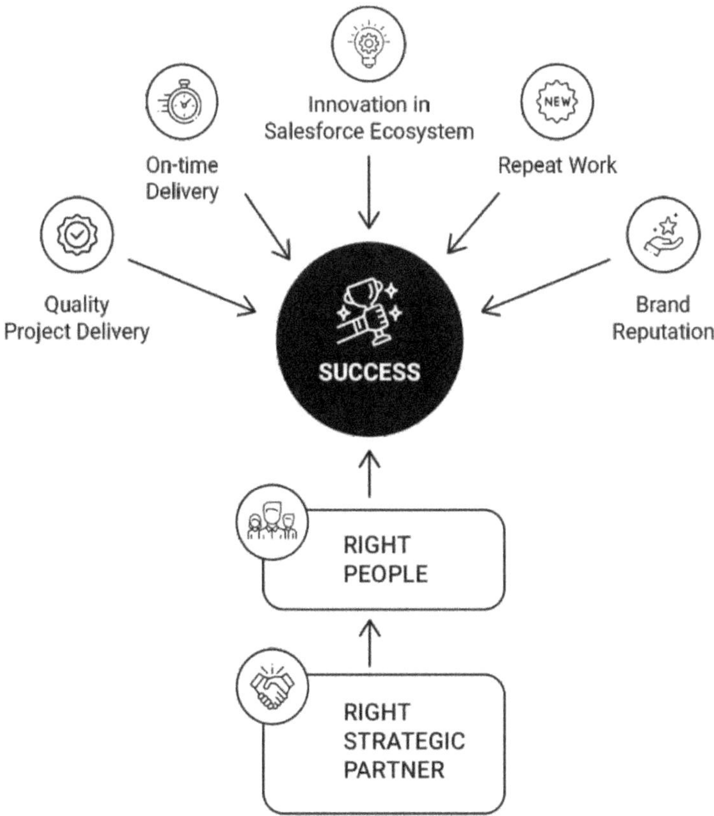

What does a business even want?

You're thinking, "Growth, I guess?"

Growth? That comes from quality project delivery, timely delivery, getting things right the first time, upholding your own brand of service and reputation, and innovating in the Salesforce ecosystem.

All of this comes from having the right people in the right place at the right time?

Now you're asking,
"All right then, how do I get the right people?"

You'll be able to source the right people on time with the right strategic partner.

"And how do I find this magical, right-as-rain strategic partner."

The right strategic partner is not some princess in a castle. There are no dragons to fight. The right partner is also not a rare flower growing on top of a huge ice-capped mountain. No mountaineering is needed.

You just need to follow the **SSA 2.0** framework.

Chapter 6: The Secret Weapon Expained

So, what even is 'Strategic Staff Aug 2.0?'

To understand and appreciate Strategic Staff Aug 2.0 more clearly, you first need to understand 2 types of partners: Transactional Staffing Partners and Strategic Staffing Partners. While Transactional partners simply provide you a resource for a price without regard for certifications and skill, a Strategic partner does things differently. The latter makes your project vision their vision.

They take care of onboarding, offboarding, paperwork, and feedback. Depending on the goals of the project, they either select the most suited person or create dream teams for the desired project outcome. They're flexible with the resources they provide. After discussions with you, they strategically combine senior technical leads and junior resources under a variety of staffing models (which we cover in greater detail in section 6. b.4.)

And therein, lies the problem.

For the past few years, I've seen partners struggling to make it in the Salesforce industry. SI firms that had taken on the wrong staffing partnerships were losing money left and right. Sincere and promising firms that could've been the Big Four for SaaS were stuck in loops instead of growth cycles.

That is precisely what Strategic Staff Aug 2.0 aims to address comprehensively. It's like a modern standard of bare minimums for a useful Salesforce partner.

Staff 2.0 is a framework that firms can use to select the right talent staffing and staff augmentation partners for them.

It's built on three core areas of evaluation:

- Salesforce Partner Credentials,
- Trust and Credibility,
- And Value Addition.

You can evaluate Strategic resource partners by asking questions before onboarding a Staff Augmentation partner about a number of parameters.

As an analogy, this is similar to how Intel's Evo-certified range of laptops needs to cross certain performance benchmarks to

be considered a competent thin and light laptop. It's also the same as how USB 3.0 needs to exceed certain minimum data transfer and charging speeds.

6.1. Salesforce Partner Credentials

Onboarding a wrong partner can be a reputation killer.

Sometimes the client is looking to fulfill immediate needs instead of doing some research about the partner. Partners should be competent enough to help the client in their growth vision. Although a 20-30 mins interaction will let you judge people by their technical skills, other key factors are overlooked in such a rushed engagement.

There are other equally (if not more) important parameters to consider which aren't immediately tangible like responsibility, cultural fit, and passion for service.

These can only come from the trust a resourcing partner builds.

There are certain parameters to look at before onboarding a Partner:

- They should have a presence in the Salesforce ecosystem for more than 7 years which indicates stability.
- At a minimum, the partners should be Salesforce Gold Consulting Partners as this requires an exhaustive eligibility criterion for credibility.
- Credentials and certifications are must-haves to show strength and seriousness towards the growth and innovation in the ecosystem.
- The partner's major technology focus should be Salesforce only.

- Multi-Cloud expertise in Salesforce is a necessity as everything moves towards the Customer 360 experience in Salesforce.
  All customers eventually ask for this, but it requires niche skills and expertise in each Salesforce Cloud.
- The firm should be engaged in Salesforce consulting services so it can train resources on real-time projects for useful exposure which helps clients.
- A sizable number of total resources and available bench pool every week is essential to expand teams and onboard resources rapidly.
- Resources at every level in the hierarchy, starting from Developers right up to Architects, should be available.
- An active and ongoing upskilling program is vital for a firm to evolve its resources and add value to the bench pool.
- Processes need to be in place to support the team whenever they fall behind or need a push to grow, like a mentor-mentee program.
- A Single Point of Contact should handle all of the client's concerns, instead of communicating with different people for each concern.
- Escalation metrics and resolution time to handle critical escalation situations should be transparently explained.
- The partner should have a strong HR foundation to hire people from the market, train them, and retain them for long.
- Emergency Replacement of onboarded resources should be provided to avoid impact on the delivery of the customer's project.

- Partners should not only be capable of sourcing specified Salesforce talent but also form a complete team of niche talents for the client to deploy on the project including Business Analysts, Product Managers, Architects, Developers, and Quality Assurance Experts.
- They should commit to non-poaching of your hard-won clients through a contract, acting as a white-labeled partner under your brand name.

Once you are done asking these questions, round out your due diligence by speaking to your partner's client for feedback.

Be sure to probe deeply and ask all necessary questions like:

"How long have you worked with them?"
"How many of their resources are currently placed?"
"What skill sets did you hire for?"
"Did you get a choice in the resources you wanted?"

Being a staffing partner myself, I work closely on my clients' growth plans and I train my teams specifically for them to acquire any desired skill set required by a project. Executing successful delivery on behalf of

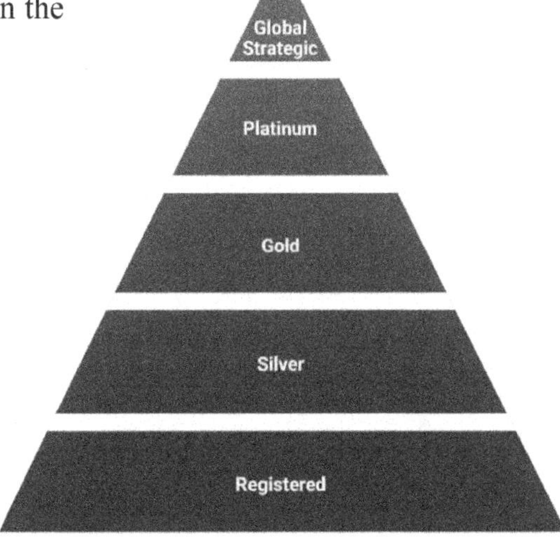

THE SECRET WEAPON EXPLAINED

my Salesforce SI clients and upholding their reputation is of the highest importance.

Here are some green flags you should look out for when checking Salesforce credentials.

6.1.1. A Consulting Company, not a Hiring Agency

Are you taking countless interviews and rejecting resources left and right?

If you can't even skip the hiring cycle and get reliable, standardized resources and skillsets in one go, then what's even the point of working with a staff augmentation partner? How is it any better than a hiring agency?

That said, a hiring agency doesn't evaluate, train, or retain a candidate pool which is the most powerful tool in an SI partner's arsenal for certain growth.

Such a candidate pool is what lets SI partners like you win and follow through on projects confidently and consistently. It lets you concentrate on consulting and earns you a reputation for quality.

Consulting companies train the resources in-house on live projects where they develop Their skills working on projects for a Specific cloud in a supervised environment under a coach or mentor, much like a dojo.

This is how resources get opportunities to choose an area of interest and build true expertise in their niche. They may also grow into T-shaped professionals - generalists with a specialization in one area. This is where they become consultants, team leads, techno-functional experts, integration experts, and more.

You should only trust partners that know how to nurture competent and reliable resources that are perfect fits for their assigned projects.

6.1.2. Dedicated Client Engagement Managers

Are you struggling with multiple points of contact with your SI partner?

The partner should offer one dedicated person to handle all the concerns related to anything like resource requirements, escalation, training, weekly status reports, and feedback.

There should be an escalation metric for all senior points of contact so that you can reach out to them in case things are not on the track with the SPOC.

6.1.3. Certified Resources

This is one of the important parameters to onboard a resource from the partner because certifications can indicate areas of interest and expertise in a field.

Let's assume you are in the market for a Salesforce Marketing Cloud expert and the resource offered by the resource partner has a Salesforce Cloud Consultant certification only.

Your alarm bells should go off at this point.

Such a mismatched resource can be a reputation spoiler and impact the delivery, for sure. Why take such risks in the first place and jeopardize client relationships?

6.1.4. Niche Skill-Set Hiring

Does your partner have expertise in different Clouds of Salesforce?

Salesforce is evolving every day and new releases are rolled out thrice a year.

Your resource partner must have expertise in niche Salesforce Clouds too and train the team on every new feature release of Salesforce.

This would also ensure that the resource partner continuously expands his/ her universe of declarative solutions.

My recommendation to all firms working for a Salesforce SI as resource partners or looking for a resource partner themselves is that they should have the above-mentioned credentials. It's a win-win situation and unlocks growth both ways for both parties.

Ultimately, my mission is to Band-Aid these bleeding wounds and provide much more value to clients than just the resources they pay for.

6.2. Trust and Credibility

This is the most common challenge for the clients where they start losing their trust in partners after being fooled by them. There are many key places where partners fool or cheat their clients.

6.2.1. Bait and Switch - Shadow Resourcing

This is a challenge where 1 resource is assigned to multiple clients at the same time without the SI partner knowing. The resource partner itself assigns some less experienced resources quietly with senior or hired resources only involved in end-client meetings and management.

The end client gets cheated out of the full value they are paying for.

6.2.2. Sitting Idle

I have heard a lot about this challenge from the SI partners at the time of the initial conversation. They complain that they want the resource to behave and work just like them.

Normally, at an SI firm when an in-house employee has no work assigned to perform, then everyone expects him/ her to inform their project managers and request more work. But at times, you'll notice that some resources prefer to sit idle instead of doing some other work for their company job - these are paid hours being wasted.

6.2.3. White Labeling

Many staffing partners are trying to showcase their own identity separately instead of showing a united front under the SI partner that employs them, which is completely unethical.

They may walk away with credit for good work and throw the SI partner under the bus for any hiccups and bad delivery. This is an ill-intentioned breach of contract and the staffing partner may try to swipe the end client from the SI partner by contacting them on their own.

6.2.4. Bait and Switch - Overcharging

Many resourcing partners try to be very competitive in the rates initially to get an SI firm hooked, but after placing a couple of resources and creating a dependency to have the SI at their mercy, the resourcing partner may start overcharging.

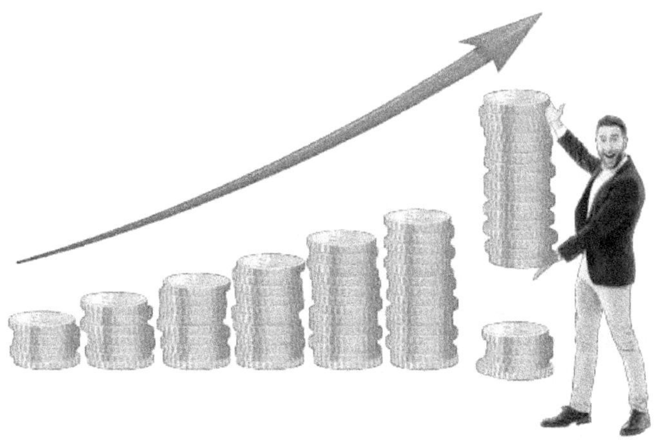

THE SECRET WEAPON EXPLAINED

6.2.5. Fake Interviews

This is another common challenge in the market where someone else gives the interview to the client in place of the actual resource. The resource gets selected based on someone else's skill and fails to deliver the desired output.

This nearly ensures that the SI firm's reputation will be ruined in front of its end-clients.

6.2.6. Fake Timesheets

We all understand that time taken to finish a job can vary from resource to resource, based on their years of experience. But some partners inflate the time for each task in the timesheet so that they can charge extra money to the clients.

Clients are falsely charged more money than they owe and this accumulates over time in the total project cost.

THE SECRET WEAPON EXPLAINED

6.2.7. Fake Experience

To bill clients higher, many resourcing partners inflate the years of experience of their resources so they can charge you at the rates of a premium resource.

Every human being has some key qualities which they carry into work and business. Such deception reflects directly on the senior management and ownership of such an SI partner.

That's why, as a coach and Salesforce partner, my core qualities are important to me as a person. I can never break anyone's trust, and neither should you - be it your girlfriend, wife, kids, family, friends, or Client.

Trust is something that takes time to build and it takes nothing to break.

And it always starts at the top.

If your staffing partner is not trustworthy then s/ he can never be a part of your journey in the long run. Their contributions to your growth will be half-hearted and shaky.

But maybe this sounds too lofty a promise.

So, I'm taking the liberty to share some real-time examples of what trust sounds like from my own clients:

" Rohit,

I have an urgent requirement for an integration expert. My own expert went on medical emergency leave.

I'll need one by today itself.

Please arrange, I know you'll never say NO to me."

"Hi Rohit,

I need 2 Vlocity experts and I have no panel to evaluate them, so just give me your best ones like you always do."

"Rohit,

I need 20 resources for my upcoming project and have no time to interview them. Highlight as many as you can to hire directly.

I'll just take your word on this."

THE SECRET WEAPON EXPLAINED

In the previous chapter, I talked about the first two core criteria of evaluating an ideal SI Partner.

In this chapter, I am sharing insights on the third:
Value Addition. Read on.

It'll tell you what a staffing partnership should
really get you.

6.3. Value Addition - Will they walk that Extra Mile?

Personally, I believe in working hand-in-hand, so I talk to my clients frequently and discuss the challenges they are facing to try and resolve them. We do this for all the resources the client onboards to ensure challenges won't keep springing up.

But many partners are very rigid in their processes and do not come out of their comfort zone to work on the custom requirement of individual clients.

It's the many little staffing and HR practices that eventually make a dream team work well and succeed in a project. And these don't happen overnight.

So, to take the guesswork out, I've spelled out the bare minimums that every resourcing partner should consciously and continuously meet.

These account for areas of value-addition like skill development, resource quality, resource availability, team models, and effective communication.

THE SECRET WEAPON EXPLAINED

6.3.1. Skill Development

6.3.1. a) Upskilling and Training

Always choose the resource partner whose main focus is on upskilling their teams. Ideally, they should take feedback from each resource and can conduct special training for them if they are found lacking somewhere in satisfying project needs.

The training could be on a wide range of topics:

- Any Salesforce technical topic,
- Salesforce's many cloud products,
- Industry knowledge,
- Interpersonal skills, Email etiquette,
- Team management,
- Project ethics,
- 1:1 mentorship for guidance,
- Salesforce Admin training,
- or new Salesforce releases

6.3.1.b) 'Skip Sessions'

These are sessions that senior managers at a resource partner firm should have with their resources about the work they are doing to gather feedback about their key challenges.

In most cases, they find that resources are not so comfortable in sharing their weaknesses or if they are lacking technically somewhere.

It's up to partners to make their resources comfortable enough to start sharing their challenges. It's at this point where they can be helped via training, mentorship, or if s/he is not comfortable with anything from the client's end.

This is what builds trust and transparency between the SI partner and the end client through feedback and longer retention of teams.

6.3.2. Resource Quality

6.3.2. a) Trustworthy Evaluation - Not just 'Hire and Place'

Make sure that you, as an SI Partner, don't need to pull the weight of the Recruitment Partner. Although hiring talent from the market is a process, placing them directly to the clients without having them evaluated is a crime.

SI firms may end up wasting time cross-evaluating recruits themselves.

You are working with the partner because you have faith in their quality commitments. So, the resource that is coming to your project must be internally evaluated for technical skills and cultural fit before approving them for a project at an end client.

Another drawback of this model is that hiring and placing directly from the market may let those applicants clear a 'fake interview' who would later fail to deliver.

6.3.3. b) Background verification: Are you sure you are not getting fooled?

This is the most common scam. Even respectable partners mention and validate fake experiences for their resources. So take nothing at face value.

Make sure you ask for a thorough background verification from an authorized agency, only to ensure that no fake resource is onboarded.

6.3.2. c) 'Proven' Experience: Is it all just talk?

Whenever we evaluate something, we look for results and factual proof to ascertain that the service or product is the best. In much the same way,  every client has all the right to ask for evidence of work, and rightfully so. These include testimonials, case studies, and referrals that speak about the partner.

6.3.2. d) Is the team evolving with Salesforce?

Here is the best way to evaluate a resource partner's commitment to growth: check how often they keep themselves updated with the new releases, technology, and emerging clouds of Salesforce.

Evaluating just basic Admin and Apex-related questions is very limiting and gives poor results. That shows that no one in the project cares about major feature updates in Salesforce, where they can be used, and how they're better than the solutions that came before them.

Once again, this puts the onus of evaluating resources on the SI partner instead of the resource partner who should be updating resources at their end.

6.3.2. e) Cost is just one factor: Do you select resource partners by cost alone?

If this is the only parameter that you are evaluating in a resource partner, then you have only yourself to blame for the blunders they commit in the project.

Oh, and did I mention this isn't a victimless crime?
Bad resources are more expensive than quality hires.

I hope I don't have to remind you that project failure comes with the loss of money, time, clients, and brand reputation. You end up paying a large, insidious cost in the long run. The quality compromise and trade-off for low prices simply aren't worth it.

6.3.2. f) There is no panacea - look for the Right Skill-set

The same medicine doesn't work for all flu types. Then why settle for a mediocre Salesforce Skill Set for every kind of project?

It is your right to ask for a niche skill set if your project demands innovative business processes and Salesforce solutions for the end client.

You may face several such situations as an SI Partner:

- Maybe your project demands a techno-functional guy that can think out of the box and can map business requirements to Salesforce solutions exactly.

- A project may need someone who can talk to the end client for close collaboration and contribute to their vision, but not all developers are up to this.

- Some projects demand constant team interaction and sprints, which needs fluent communication.

- If you need someone that can handle teams too, then the resource should have team management capabilities along with technical skills.

6.3.3.) Resource Availability

6.3.3. a) Resource Replacement

Isn't it reassuring to have a warranty on your resources?

My own SI partners sleep like babies, secure in the knowledge that if a resource doesn't work out, s/he can be replaced.

If you have onboarded a resource that isn't capable enough to perform a job or lacks in a skill set, a great partner would immediately minimize your losses by switching out the resource for a better one.

But good luck doing that if the partner has you in a rigid contract.

Because then, you're stuck paying for a sub-par resource for the rest of the project.

6.3.3. b.) Resource Retention

Training resources for a project is an expensive, yet necessary affair.

The market for Salesforce developers is super competitive at this time [mid-2022.] This makes it even more important for resource partners to know how to retain resources instead of fishing for new resources every week that you need to train from ground zero.

Also, you can no longer write off employee satisfaction as a nice-to-have. It's a full-blown, 24x7 operation that only a few partners do well at.

6.3.3. c) Back-Up Resources

The partner should be capable enough to provide you with the backup of any resource with a similar skill set in case of an emergency.

Lack of backup resources is a loss for the client because they end up working with a resource who gets comfortable with the project and the client may have spent time training the resource on their systems.

We all understand that emergencies happen and smaller absences can be managed, but they can be planned for in advance and should be avoided.

Even in such scenarios, a resource partner should be able to provide you with backup resources for a specific period.

6.3.3. d) Ad-hoc Resources and Consultants

There are many situations where clients could need a consultant, architect, or developer on an ad-hoc basis like:

- Delivering a stalled project,
- Getting a second or third opinion,

- or an ongoing large-scale project that needs more teams and senior leads.

Partners should be open to this, and most importantly, they must have experts in their organization who can be called on at a moment's notice to contribute.

Sometimes, clients require additional expertise, such as AppExchange app creation, solution design, architecture design, and MVP creation. Solutions also need to be designed dynamically so they can be customized to any Salesforce Org.

6.3.4. Resource Team Models

A variety of hiring models could be used by a strategic resource partner to fulfill this requirement for extra expertise:

6.3.4. a) Project Team

These are bespoke teams with a combination of a variety of roles like BA, QA, Admin, specialist developers, and architects.

6.3.4. b) Horse and Cart Model

This is a cost-effective team model which combines the advantages of a senior resource, multiple developers working parallelly, and a manageable hierarchical structure. A senior tech lead (horse) pulls and ensures performance from junior developers (carts), that work as a team with high productivity and are easier to manage with less lead devs (horses).

This model is only applicable when the client is looking for a big team and has challenges in onboarding talent. As a popular model, the partner should discuss this plan very clearly with the client instead, or else they might resort to fake interviews or shadow resourcing.

The clients hiring resources understand market pains and the need for such models. They know that getting all the 'horses' on the project sometimes is neither possible nor cost-effective. But the partner should be trustworthy and transparent about their approach too.

So, partners should be capable and innovative to discuss with the client to build a team where they can add some horses (Tech leads) along with some junior developers who can support in building the project.

6.3.4. c) Train and Deploy

In this model, a batch of Resources is specially trained on a chosen technology and industry. It is then deployed through a contract. This is a good option for you as an SI partner when you're looking for specific resource quantities for a project where the technology or industry is very niche.

6.3.5. Communication

6.3.5. a) Weekly Status Reports (WSR)

As mentioned earlier, there should be SPOC (Single Point of Contact) i.e., a Client Engagement manager that shares a weekly status report with the client. The report should include the risk areas where the client needs to look into or intervene.

Clients need to check:

- If any resource doesn't have the work or tasks assigned to them
- If a resource plans to go on leave
- How many resources are onboarded in the previous week
- How many interviews were conducted in the previous week
- Updated resource requirements shared by the client
- If there are any outstanding finance-related concerns
- The shared list of resources beforehand
- In case their contract renewal is approaching
- Updates on escalations, if any
- The status of resource training, in case it is conducted upon special request of the client

6.3.5. b) Daily Timesheet Updates

The resource working for the client should share daily updates with their manager on the Client-side and should fill the timesheet either at the Client's end or in their current organization. This puts to rest any trust issues that may snowball into bigger challenges later.

By doing so,

- There will be transparency on what tasks a resource is working on
- Idle resources are quickly identified and added back to the bench pool, and the possibility of inflating timesheets is eliminated
- If the resource is lacking in the skill, then the manager (at the end client) is alerted and can ask for a replacement
- The client will get greater confidence in timely and quality-checked delivery of projects

6.3.5.c) Real-time Communication

Is communication a challenge with offshore resource partners?

We all understand that communication is the key for every business or work, so it is super important that the resource which is going to work with the client should be available in their time zone.

This helps facilitate communication and resolve any issues at the same time so end-clients can:

- Communicate with the team for any major concerns at once
- Ask questions or help within minutes
- Review and give feedback on tasks at the same time
- Frequently chat with the team for any brainstorming sessions
- Demo and test finished solutions immediately

"It's like a weight has been lifted since I've started working with 360. I finally have a partner with round-the-clock resource coverage.

No more getting up at 5 am to get just a few minutes with an offshore resource. I've finally got my time-freedom back and can concentrate on my family and business."

Here's a summary of the key questions you need to ask before hiring resources from any platform or agency to ensure they meet Strategic Staff Aug 2.0:

1) Are you working with Salesforce Summit (Platinum) Partners?
2) Is your Salesforce Partner in existence for more than 7 years in the Salesforce ecosystem?
3) Does your partner have strong Credentials and Certifications?
4) Does your partner work only with Salesforce?
5) Are they a hiring company or a consulting company?
6) Do they offer a big bench Pool of resources to expand?
7) Are they working with any Big 4 or Fortune 500 companies?
8) Is your partner offering a niche skill set or specific Salesforce cloud expertise?
9) Is your partner giving you dedicated resources (SPOC)?
10) Is your partner providing the resource in your time-zone?
11) Is your partner evolving with Salesforce?
12) Is your partner trustworthy and honest?

But the best solution is to hire a Strategic Resource Partner that meets the Strategic Staff Aug 2.0 criteria. Such partners beat every other option - hiring agency and freelancing portals - hands-down. They beat rock, paper, scissors, everything.

That's because they'll always give you the most growth.

Chapter 7: How They Did It

Phew! That was a long piece of strategic advice. I hope you got the value you were hoping for. Now, let's see how companies like yours have achieved their strategic objectives.

Let's begin with the first case study…

Case Study 1:

A mega Salesforce partner transforms project delivery and meets a surge in demand with SSA 2.0

The first case study is about BigX [name changed] - one of the 4 largest SI partners with one of the world's largest digital transformation practices. It has a huge presence in the Salesforce ecosystem which accounts for a large chunk of its revenue.

The problem began during the pandemic, offline took a huge hit, and every business was moving operations to SaaS platforms. As the world's #1 CRM, Salesforce got the best sales during this time with a large number of businesses counting on it for growth. Salesforce needed partners to customize its CRM for these customers, which meant a huge pipeline of projects also came to Big X.

Now that new customers were onboarded, it was time to implement the projects. All teams swung into action and started with resource planning, during which, they found themselves short of resources up against the demands and tight delivery timelines they were facing.

Even with one of the largest Salesforce teams in the world, time was running out and there were deadlines to meet. It had in-house teams in place to take on these projects but due to the unusually high volume of onboarded projects, this wouldn't be nearly enough.

As a standard response, the delivery managers turned to the talent acquisition and procurement teams for 2 things:

- Hiring more in-house resources, for which specifications were shared.
- Onboarding more Salesforce partners.

That's when Big X ran into problems.

On one end, the talent acquisition realized from forecasting that they were looking at a lengthened 4-6 month hiring cycle for the in-house team, which meant they wouldn't be able to fulfill in-house hiring needs in time. This would also be a compromise on resource quality.

This was because there had been a boom in the Salesforce ecosystem and IT market at large. Other large firms had closed many deals during the pandemic too. This spurred high attrition everywhere and caused a resource crunch. Prices had also soared to unprecedented levels.

On the other hand, the procurement team was able to onboard a few Salesforce partners and get resources, but soon ran into some issues.

Smaller vendors weren't as competent and harder to keep track of in multiples. They never had quality resources which meant resources were poorly mapped. Resumes were window-dressed and resources would never live up to their skills on paper.

Resource availability was also always a problem: senior resources were shadowing for other projects; talent pools were always smaller and couldn't accommodate bandwidth; multi-cloud specialization was hard to come by.

And even when resources we finally onboarded, they would get changed frequently after spending many months in KT (knowledge transfer), so projects would start from scratch.

Eventually, everything was a silent compromise with these Salesforce partners, which led to frustrations.

The magical shift happened when Big X first met Rohit as a strategic partner who introduced them to **the SSA 2.0 framework.**

Rohit worked with Big X under a strategic partnership on SSA 2.0 Principles.

This is when things turned around for Big X.

It was through SSA 2.0, that Rohit helped Big X analyze and understand where it burned the most cash, what it could get for the same money, and where it could be allocated for better value. This led to 360 DC being onboarded.

HOW THEY DID IT

This resulted in access to a large bench pool that met its huge demand for resources, suitable resourcing strategies and models were implemented, and any challenges along the way became manageable with a competent partner, so they were met head-on.

Delivery teams were happier that they now need only ask for resources, however niche, and they would be available.

BigX's project delivery had completely transformed with a host of big improvements.

- The huge demand for resources was met
- Achieved better resource-project fit
- Faster, Reliable Project Delivery
- Cost-effective Resource Models
- Better Pipeline Visibility, Workforce Management

The SSA 2.0 framework delivered on all its promises, even through one of the toughest challenges of our time - Covid 19. **This was the start of a transformative growth relationship that's still going strong.**

The partners now enjoy a warm, reliable relationship built on trust and transparency. Big X knows it has a steadfast partner in Rohit that can just get things done.

Case Study 2:

A UK-based Salesforce SI finds reliable resource partners with SSA 2.0, takes on bigger accounts

The second case study is about SalesPro [name changed] a renowned Salesforce Platinum partner in the UK that worked strictly locally. But soon the partner increasingly found itself handling big accounts.

So they thought it was finally time to impanel some outsourcing partners for Salesforce resources, though reluctantly.

The Problem began, facing a resource crunch once bigger customers came in so they decided to partner with some offshore vendors.

Soon enough, SalesPro ran into some challenges.

On top of overcharging for resources and then shadowing them for other projects, the quality of resources provided by these offshore partners was also quite poor. They could never seem to fulfill demands satisfactorily.

This put SalesPro in a bind. Impaneling a partner is a time-taking process that stretches for months, so when a partner being impaneled isn't able to honor deliveries, the impaneling process would need to start all over.

HOW THEY DID IT

The setback and the loss incurred by SalesPro left them soured on the idea of offshore partners.

It was around this time that SalesPro met Rohit through its digital networks. Having burnt themselves already, it was hard for SalesPro to put its faith in outsourcing to Salesforce partners again.

Leading a Platinum Partner of Salesforce, Rohit assured the procurement and practice heads of CRM while also introducing them to the SSA 2.0 framework.

It was here that they were first introduced to and adopted the **SSA 2.0 framework**. Implementing the framework took a few months but paid off richly.

This helped SalesPro to find the right resources at the right time with better resource mapping.

Specialized multi-cloud resources were also provided, along with better team configurations and resource models.

They were 8 resources (1 Tech Lead, 1 Technical Architect, and 6 Developers) under a **horse-and-cart resource model**. In addition to this, they were also provided a business analyst and quality assurance analyst to support development operations.

Once this team was deployed out in the field, SalesPro tasted success. It won even more projects and repeat work. And as they closed and launched more projects on time, they also onboarded a dedicated resource for go-live support.

SalesPro now operated under a framework and management regained confidence after a string of setbacks from its outsourced partners. The firm was no longer tied down to low-quality vendors and flipped its outsourcing partnership completely.

With SSA 2.0, all resource requirements were fulfilled in time and operated as closely as an in-house team.

The firm is now comfortable picking up larger, more demanding projects which would bolster its portfolio and help it grow.

Chapter 8: Your Key to 4x Salesforce Practice Growth

You now understand, in greater depth, the invisible problems and costs holding your business to ransom.

You've also understood the SSA 2.0 framework approach and why it's central to modern resourcing strategy.

You're thinking, "But does it end here Rohit?"
I'm afraid it doesn't.

Even if you do implement the framework, how do you know you're tapping into its full potential? Do you now want to know how other businesses have implemented this? Do you want to see case studies of how this has worked out for other businesses? That's where you need to be proactive.

You'll be caught up in project deliveries again with the next phone call tomorrow, neck-deep in stalled or prolonged projects. Finding a strategic partner takes time. You will need to pull yourself away from many ongoing engagements and urgent notifications.

And now that you've come so far, I don't want you to fail.

So, let's sit across each other at a table and connect.

Let's unlock success for your organization together.

I would love nothing more in this world than to craft a strategy that's unique to your Salesforce practice.

NOTES

NOTES

NOTES

NOTES

NOTES

NOTES

NOTES

NOTES

NOTES

NOTES